THE SCIENCE OF
NUTRITION

WHY WE NEED

· ·

PROTEINS

By Angela Royston

Crabtree Publishing Company

www.crabtreebooks.com

Crabtree Publishing Company

www.crabtreebooks.com

Author: Angela Royston
Publishing plan research and development:
  Sean Charlebois, Reagan Miller
Editors: Sarah Eason, Nick Hunter, Lynn Peppas
Proofreaders: Robyn Hardyman, Kathy Middleton
Project coordinator: Kathy Middleton
Design: Calcium
Photo Research: Susannah Jayes
Print coordinator: Katherine Berti
Production coordinator and prepress technician:
  Ken Wright
Series consultant: Julie Negrin

Library and Archives Canada Cataloguing in Publication

Royston, Angela
    Why we need proteins / Angela Royston.

(The science of nutrition)
Includes index.
Issued also in electronic format.
ISBN 978-0-7787-1689-1 (bound).--ISBN 978-0-7787-1696-9 (pbk.)

    1. Proteins in human nutrition--Juvenile literature.
I. Title. II. Series: Science of nutrition (St. Catharines, Ont.)

QP551.R69 2011   j612'.01575   C2011-900209-4

Library of Congress Cataloging-in-Publication Data

Royston, Angela, 1945-
  Why we need proteins / Angela Royston.
     p. cm. -- (The science of nutrition)
  Includes index.
  ISBN 978-0-7787-1696-9 (pbk. : alk. paper) -- ISBN 978-0-7787-1689-1
  (reinforced library binding : alk. paper) -- ISBN 978-1-4271-9680-4
  (electronic (pdf))
  1. Proteins in human nutrition--Juvenile literature. I. Title. II. Series.

  QP551.R868 2011
  612.3'98--dc22

                                        2010052768

Crabtree Publishing Company

www.crabtreebooks.com   1-800-387-7650

Printed in the U.S.A./022011/CJ20101228

Published in Canada
Crabtree Publishing
616 Welland Ave.
St. Catharines, Ontario
L2M 5V6

Published in the United States
Crabtree Publishing
PMB 59051
350 Fifth Avenue, 59th Floor
New York, New York 10118

Published in the United Kingdom
Crabtree Publishing
Maritime House
Basin Road North, Hove
BN41 1WR

Published in Australia
Crabtree Publishing
386 Mt. Alexander Rd.
Ascot Vale (Melbourne)
VIC 3032

CONTENTS

FOOD FOR FUEL

When you eat a cheese sandwich you might think you are just eating bread, cheese, and lettuce, but you are eating much more than that. Hidden inside your food are important nutrients that you need to stay alive and healthy.

You need nutrients

This book is about protein. The other main **nutrients** are **carbohydrates** and fats, but you also need tiny amounts of nutrients called vitamins and minerals. You have to eat enough—but not too much—of each kind of nutrient to stay healthy. Luckily, each nutrient is found in many different foods, so you can choose healthful food that you like.

The same mix of foods is not right for everyone. Children need a slightly different mix of foods than adults as their bodies are growing.

The food pyramid shows healthy foods only. It does not include foods such as cookies and chips, which are high in salt, fat, or sugar.

Grains
Grains give you energy, but they also contain some protein and other nutrients.

Vegetables and fruits
You should eat a wide range from these two groups to get all the nutrients you need.

Oils and fats
These foods should not be overeaten.

Milk
This group of foods is rich in protein but can also be high in fat.

Meat and beans
These foods are rich in protein, although meats can also be high in fat.

Essential protein

There are thousands of different proteins in your body. Each one does a specific job. Some proteins help to build and repair the body's cells. Others speed up all the **chemical reactions** that go on inside the body. There are also proteins that carry chemicals around the body and help fight infection.

Protein from food

The food pyramid divides healthy foods into six groups. Choosing food from each of these groups will give you all the nutrients you need.

WHAT IS PROTEIN?

Every part of you, from your toenails to the hairs on your head, is made of different proteins. Your body needs a constant supply of them to grow bigger, and to repair and replace existing cells. Proteins are made of smaller building blocks called amino acids.

Children grow taller and heavier. They can only do so because their bodies add millions of new cells to their bones, muscles, and other parts of their bodies.

Starting out

You began life as a single cell that split and divided again and again to form the billions of cells that make up your body now. Each cell is responsible for carrying out a special job. For example, the heart consists of heart cells, which pump blood around your body. Your muscles consist of muscle cells, which move your body. Your bones are made up of cells that help support your body.

Making new cells

Your body needs protein to make new cells. You make most new cells when you are young and still growing, but everyone makes new cells to replace those that have died. Brain cells last your entire life, but most cells die much faster. Each red blood cell, for example, lasts only about four months. Your body produces more than a million new red blood cells every second to replace the dead cells.

Did you know?

The cells in the lining of the stomach last only a few days before they are destroyed by the acid in your stomach.

Your body replaces old cells constantly, in every part of your body from your hair, skin, and teeth to your eyes, mouth, and fingernails. Your body requires protein to do this.

The **germ**, or center, of a whole grain
has proteins. The germ has a lot of
amino acids that the plant has made.

Building proteins

A molecule is the smallest part of
something that can exist. Compared with
most other molecules, protein molecules
are very large and complicated. They are
made of strings of amino acids that are
joined together in different ways.

There are thousands of different proteins,
but they are all different combinations of
just 20 amino acids. Some proteins contain
thousands of amino acids linked together.

Body Talk

Amino acids are
needed to help the
body repair itself.
Not having the right
amino acids can leave
your body unable to repair
itself from injury or illness.

Did you know?

Plants are amino acid factories. They manufacture all the amino acids they need from chemicals in the air and in the water they take in from the soil. Animals eat plants or other animals to get amino acids and other nutrients. People get amino acids from eating animals and plants.

The body can make some amino acids itself. The amino acids the body can make are called inessential amino acids. There are nine amino acids that the body cannot make or cannot make enough of. These are called essential amino acids. The only way you can get essential amino acids is from the foods you eat. Most of this protein comes from animal food products such as meat and eggs. A few plants, such as soybeans, also contain a lot of protein.

Many people blame the amino acid tryptophan (found in turkey meat) for feeling sleepy after they eat Thanksgiving dinner. But, tryptophan only makes you sleepy if it is taken on an empty stomach. That tired feeling comes from eating too much good food!

PROTEIN FOODS

Many foods contain some protein. Some foods, however, are very rich in protein. A food that provides all the essential amino acids is called a complete protein. Meat and fish are complete proteins and can easily provide all the protein you need each day.

Types of meat

Beef, lamb, and pork come from cows, sheep, and pigs and are called red meat. People eat many different parts of animals, including the liver and heart, but the most common forms of meat come from the muscles. Muscles from different parts of the animals are chopped up to make meat that we roast, grill, or stew.

Meat that comes from birds, such as chicken and turkey, is known as white meat. White meat generally has less fat than red meat. But beware! Crispy, fried chicken or turkey gravy can add unneeded fat and calories.

The best source of protein is the meat from farm animals such as sheep and cows. The meat is the muscles of the animal.

> *I do not like red meat, but I eat chicken and fish to make sure I get enough protein.*

Fish are excellent sources of protein and other nutrients. Food experts suggest people eat fish at least twice a week.

Body Talk

Oily fish, such as trout, mackerel, sardines, and salmon, contain omega-3 oils, which are good for your heart and brain. Omega-3s are only found in protein-rich foods such as fish, nuts, and soybeans. Fish from fish farms contain fewer omega oils than wild fish.

Try this...

The next time you eat meat look closely at what you are eating. You will see that meat is made of many strands bundled together. The strands are muscle fibers and together they form a muscle that controlled movement in the animal from which it came.

Cow's milk provides us with a rich source of protein.

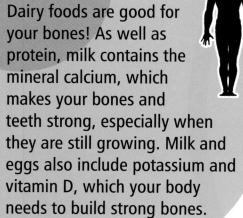

Body Talk

Dairy foods are good for your bones! As well as protein, milk contains the mineral calcium, which makes your bones and teeth strong, especially when they are still growing. Milk and eggs also include potassium and vitamin D, which your body needs to build strong bones.

Other sources of protein

All animal protein is complete protein, but you do not have to eat meat to get it. Eggs and milk come from animals, and so food made with eggs and milk contain complete proteins, too.

All about milk

You can drink milk just as it is, or you can eat it as yogurt or cheese. Cream and butter are also made from milk. Most milk that we drink in North America comes from cows, but all mammals produce milk. In many parts of the world people drink sheep, goat, and even camel milk. Some cheeses bought in North America are made from sheep milk.

What is in an egg?

Eggs can be cooked and eaten on their own or used in recipes. Almost all baked goods contain eggs. The yellow yolk contains fat as well as protein, while the part around the yolk, called the **albumen**, is pure protein.

Try this...

Break an egg into a bowl. With help from an adult, cook the egg for three minutes, either by frying it or poaching it. What happens to the albumen—the clear jelly? Cooking breaks up the amino acids. The acids form new, stronger links, which turn the clear jelly into a white solid.

I eat egg-white omelets. They are packed with protein.

Eggs are rich in animal protein. Most of the eggs we eat are hen's eggs.

Protein from plants

Cereals, nuts, seeds, and **legumes** are all plants that are rich in protein. Most plants do not contain all the essential amino acids and are called incomplete proteins. As long as you eat a variety of plant proteins throughout the day, you will get all the proteins you need.

Raw cocoa beans do not contain sugar and actually taste quite bitter. Sugar is added when the beans are made into chocolate, to make it taste sweet.

Cereals are packed with protein

Cereals, which include rice, wheat, rye, oats, barley, quinoa, and corn, produce protein-rich seeds called grains. Rice grains are mostly cooked and eaten whole. Wheat grains are ground into flour, which is made into bread, pasta, cakes, and other foods. Whole grains such as whole wheat bread are much better for you than refined grains such as the flour used in white bread. Wheat, corn, rice, and oats are all made into popular breakfast cereals.

Did you know?

Cocoa beans contain protein, which means that chocolate contains protein, too! When chocolate is refined to make candy bars, a lot of sugar is added. There is less cocoa and less protein.

Legumes deliver a protein punch

Legumes are seeds that grow in a pod, such as beans, peas, lentils, and chickpeas. They are rich in protein. Nuts, seeds, and plant oils, which are all rich in protein, are usually eaten as snacks or included in other foods.

Soybeans are one of the cheapest and most useful sources of protein. Unlike other plants, soybeans provide complete protein. Tofu is made from soybeans and can be eaten on its own or made into "meat alternatives" such as veggie burgers and soy mince.

I am a vegetarian, so I have to make sure I eat a lot of tofu and beans for protein.

A stir-fried meal often includes vegetables and protein-rich tofu.

HOW MUCH IS ENOUGH?

You might need much less protein than you think. Protein should make up only about ten to 15 percent of an adult's total diet. Protein should be about 20 percent of a child's diet. Most people eat much more protein than they actually need.

The amount of protein you need is often given in terms of the amount of food you need to eat. This is called **equivalent** protein and is easier to use than the actual weight of protein the food contains. Adult men need about six ounces (170 g) of equivalent protein a day, while children aged nine to 13 and adult women need five ounces (140 g) a day. Younger people need to eat more protein as a percentage of their diet because it helps their bodies to grow.

*Children need extra protein, especially when they are growing fast, when they are very young, and when they reach **puberty**.*

Did you know?

People who traditionally live where few plants grow often eat lots of protein. For example, the Inuit people, who live in and around the Arctic, eat mostly fish and very few vegetables.

I eat protein at every meal.

I always thought it was better to eat meat than bread, but it is not.

How much food?

One ounce (28 g) of lean meat, chicken, or fish gives one ounce of equivalent protein, so a five-ounce (140 g) chicken breast would give you all the protein you need for a day. However, most things you eat contain some protein, so you do not need to get all your protein from one portion. For example, a tablespoon (15 ml) of peanut butter provides one ounce (28 g) of equivalent protein. If you eat a healthy diet, you will easily get all the protein you need.

People need different amounts of protein at different ages.

Too much protein

Eating too much protein can lead to health problems including being overweight. If people eat too much protein, the body stores it as fat. Some doctors also think that too much protein, especially too much red meat, can lead to heart and kidney problems.

Body Talk

Muscles consist of protein, so some body builders think that eating protein helps to build their muscles, but they are probably wrong. Exercise makes the muscle fibers thicker and stronger, but this does not require much extra protein.

My dad loves steak. He eats so much protein! I do not think it is good for him.

People who like to build up large muscles will eat more and exercise. If they decrease their amount of exercise, they must be careful not to eat too much or they may become overweight.

Did you know?

In the past, rich people thought that vegetables and bread were for poor people. The rich ate huge amounts of different kinds of meat, even at the same meal. As a result many became very overweight and suffered from painful diseases such as gout.

If you eat more protein than you need, your liver converts some of it into sugar. Extra sugar means that the body stores more fat, which will make you heavier. Animal protein often contains fat, which can clog up the blood vessels in the heart.

Kidney problems

Changing amino acids into sugar produces urea, or the main liquid in waste, which your kidneys then have to get out of your body. This makes your kidneys work very hard, which can sometimes cause them not to work well. When this happens, you may get **gout**. People with gout suffer from painful joints, especially in their big toes.

Body builders train all year to build up the strength of their muscles.

This U.S. helicopter is dropping food
to starving villagers in Pakistan.

Too little protein

Millions of people in the world do
not eat enough protein. This is usually
because they are very poor and cannot
afford to buy enough food, or because
there is a shortage of food in the country
where they live.

Food that is rich in protein is often more
expensive than other food. Poor people
often have a very limited diet that contains
only a small amount of protein. Not getting
enough protein as a child may mean that
you do not grow to your full height and
have trouble fighting off disease.

Did you know?

In August 2010, the country
of Pakistan in Asia flooded. The
floods destroyed crops and farm
animals. Millions of people had
no food. The U.S. government
and aid organizations sent
emergency food to as many
people as possible. The food
had extra protein added to it
to help the people survive.

Kwashiorkor

Kwashiorkor is a **fatal**, or deadly, disease caused by an extreme lack of protein. It mostly affects children under the age of three in countries suffering from **famine**, or lack of food. The most obvious signs of kwashiorkor are thin arms and legs and a large, swollen belly. The only way to recover from kwashiorkor is to eat high-protein food. Even then, children who have had the disease will grow to be small as adults.

Many children in developing countries do not have enough to eat. The lack of protein in their diets can make them feel extremely tired and make it difficult for them to learn.

If I do not eat enough protein, I cannot think straight at school.

IT'S ON THE LABEL

Water contains no nutrients or calories but is essential for your body. Whole fat milk contains more fat than skim milk, but both contain protein and other nutrients.

Many of the foods that people buy have a mixture of ingredients, and most ingredients have a mixture of nutrients. So how do you figure out how healthy or not a food is? The answer is on the label! The label tells you exactly what is in a food product and how much of each of the main nutrients and some important vitamins and minerals it contains.

To save time, many people buy food that has already been prepared and cooked. Breakfast cereals, cans of soup, baked beans, and macaroni and cheese are just some examples of prepared food. Some of these foods look healthy, but if you check the label you may find they contain a lot of fat, salt, and sugar.

Many artificial drinks have food labels. Soda drinks, such as cola, are packed with sugar and are the least healthy drinks.

Where to look

Information about prepared, or processed, food is on the packaging. Breakfast cereals, for example, give nutritional information and ingredients on the back or on the side of the box. A candy bar has the information on the back of the bar.

Reading the labels

The list of ingredients on a food label gives the biggest ingredient first and the smallest ingredient last. The nutritional value of the food is also given. This table shows you how many calories an amount of the food will give you and how much actual protein and salt it gives. Too much salt is not good for you.

This part of a food label shows the calories, protein, and other nutrients the food contains. It also shows the amount of fat, sugar, and salt.

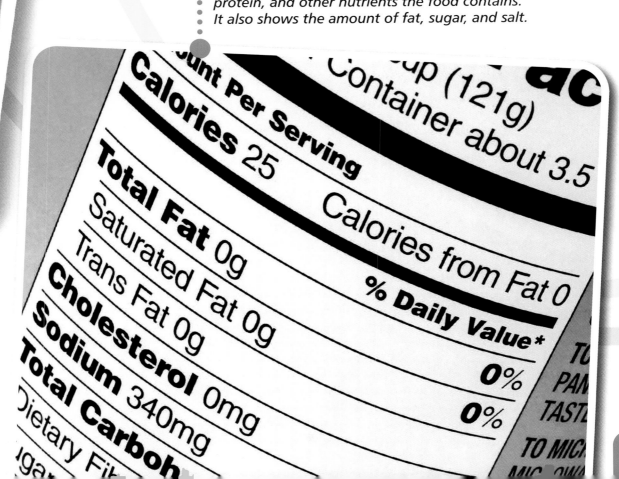

up (121g)
Container about 3.5

unt Per Serving

Calories 25   Calories from Fat 0

% Daily Value*

Total Fat 0g

Saturated Fat 0g

Trans Fat 0g

Cholesterol 0mg   **0%**

Sodium 340mg   **0%**

Total Carboh

Dietary Fi

23

Daily Values

The amounts of different nutrients are given as a percentage of the total amount that you need to eat each day. The total amounts are called the Daily Values (DV). They are based on the average amount that an adult needs. They do not take into account an individual's circumstances.

Understanding the information

The nutritional information given on a label is often a mixture of good and bad news. To find out what is going on, look at each item in the chart. Compare the amount of protein and the healthy contents, such as vitamins and fiber, with the amount of sugar and unhealthy fat, that is saturated fat and **trans fat**.

Body Talk

A serving of food is high in protein if it contributes more than 20 percent of the Daily Value. It is low in protein if it contributes less than five percent.

Beans are a great source of protein.

24

Nutritional guidelines

Food experts advise people about how much of each different nutrient people should eat. For example, they suggest that an average person needs about 2,000 calories a day to stay healthy. The nutritional information on food labels helps you stick to these guidelines. But it is important to remember not everyone is the same. Someone who plays a lot of sports will need, and burn off, more calories than the recommended guidelines.

Before you buy a packaged food because it looks healthy, check the food label. You might be surprised how much sugar, salt, and other additives the food actually contains!

Try this...

Collect a selection of prepared foods, such as baked beans, frozen pizza, and fruit yogurt. Which do you think will give you the most protein in one serving? Check the labels. Were you right?

PROTEIN BODY BUILDERS

Try this...

Your body is more than half water, and you have a layer of fat under your skin, but the rest is made up almost entirely of protein. The body uses different proteins to build different parts of the body, such as your skin, muscles, teeth, and lungs. Different proteins are made up of different combinations of amino acids. Proteins that are used to build the body are called structural proteins. **Collagen** and **keratin** are two examples of structural proteins.

Muscles move the bones and are made of protein. Athletes exercise to make their muscles strong and powerful.

A rhino's horn is mainly keratin.

Collagen is a tough protein. It is made up of bundles of fibers that do not stretch. Collagen fibers make up **cartilage** and connective tissues. Cartilage is the rubbery stuff that cushions the ends of your bones. Connective tissues hold body organs in place. The bones themselves are made mostly of collagen. They are harder than cartilage because they also contain the mineral calcium.

Your hair, nails, and the outer layer of your skin are all made of the tough protein keratin. Keratin is very strong and tough. The outer layer of your skin has to be tough to withstand all the knocks and scratches it gets.

Did you know?

Birds' feathers, animals' claws, and mammals' fur are all made of keratin. Every part of a bird's feather is made of keratin. The keratin makes the feather strong but bendy.

If I do not eat enough protein, my nails become really weak and flaky.

Working the body

Hundreds of things are going on in your body all the time. Blood flows around the body, your intestines digest food, your lungs take in air, and new cells are always being made. The body uses thousands of different proteins to perform all the processes that keep you alive. These proteins are called functional proteins. **Hemoglobin** and **antibodies** are both functional proteins that are made and carried in the blood.

Body Talk

Why is blood red? Blood consists of water and different kinds of cells, including trillions of red blood cells. You have so many red blood cells, they make your blood red. It is the red hemoglobin that makes the red blood cells red.

The functional protein hemoglobin is at work when an athlete gasps in air to replace all the oxygen his muscles have just used up.

Hemoglobin carries oxygen from your lungs to every cell in the body. Oxygen in the air you breathe in passes through the walls of the lungs into your blood. It sticks to the hemoglobin in the red blood cells until it is released and passes into a cell. Every cell in your body needs oxygen to change sugar into energy.

Blood carries functional proteins around your body to feed every living cell.

Antibodies

Antibodies are proteins that your body makes to fight disease. When you get sick, your white blood cells make antibodies that kill the germs that cause the illness. The antibodies stay in your blood, ready to attack if the same germs return.

Did you know?

Hormones are proteins that are carried in the blood. Each has a special job to do. For example, insulin made in the **pancreas** controls the amount of sugar that is present in the blood.

DIGESTION

You certainly cannot swallow a piece of pizza whole! You have to chew it one bite at a time.

The body cannot use the proteins you eat directly. They have to be first broken down into their separate amino acids, which your body then puts together again to make the proteins it needs. The job of the **digestive system** is to break up food into pieces that are so tiny they can pass through the walls of the digestive tube into your blood.

Why do we cook food?

Many foods, especially meat and fish, are cooked to make them easier to chew and to digest. Cooking meat or fish at the correct temperature kills most germs, making the food safe to eat. Cereals are usually ground and baked to make bread and other foods that you buy. Cooking softens the muscle fibers and starts to loosen the bonds between the amino acids.

Try this...

Use a fork to mash cooked rice and then raw rice. Which is easier to squash? Does it make a difference if you soak the uncooked rice for about 30 minutes? Why?

Breaking down food

The process of digestion begins in the mouth. As you chew, your teeth break up the food, which mixes with **saliva** to make a soft mush that you can swallow. Saliva is a digestive juice. It kills some of the germs and starts to break up the carbohydrates.

Body Talk

Sushi is a Japanese way of preparing food, which often includes raw fish. Cooking food kills germs. Because it is not cooked, raw fish has to be specially stored and prepared.

Some people think eating raw fish is gross, but sushi is packed with protein and is good for you.

Protein-rich oysters are not just raw, they are still alive when you swallow them!

The digestive machine

When you swallow, the food goes down your throat into a long tube, called the digestive system. As food travels through the digestive system, it is broken down into smaller and smaller pieces. Eventually, the food ends up as tiny molecules that your body can use.

First, food goes down a tube called the **esophagus** and then into the stomach. Here, it mixes with strong acids that kill any remaining germs. Gradually, the walls of the stomach squeeze and turn the food into a thick liquid called **chyme**.

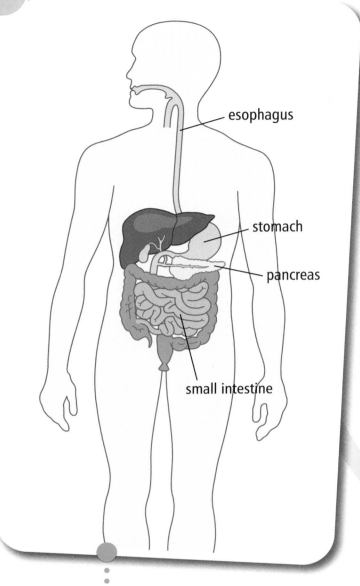

esophagus

stomach

pancreas

small intestine

Body Talk

Without **enzymes**, your intestines would have to be as hot as an oven to break down proteins and other foods. Enzymes allow the body to do the same job at about 100° Fahrenheit (37° C).

The enzyme pepsin begins to break up protein in the stomach. Enzymes in the digestive juices from the pancreas do the main work in the small intestine.

Did you know?

Your small **intestine** is more than three times as long as your whole body. An adult's intestine is 22 feet (7 m) long!

: The walls of the small intestine are
: lined with small bumps called villi.
: The walls of the villi are so thin,
: molecules of food can easily pass
: through them into the blood.

Into the small intestine

The chyme spurts into a long, thin tube called the small intestine. Here digestive juices break it up into smaller and smaller pieces. The juices contain enzymes—special proteins that break up the large protein molecules into shorter and shorter strings of amino acids. These are small enough to pass through the wall of the small intestine into the blood. The blood carries the nutrients to the liver—the next stage in the digestive journey.

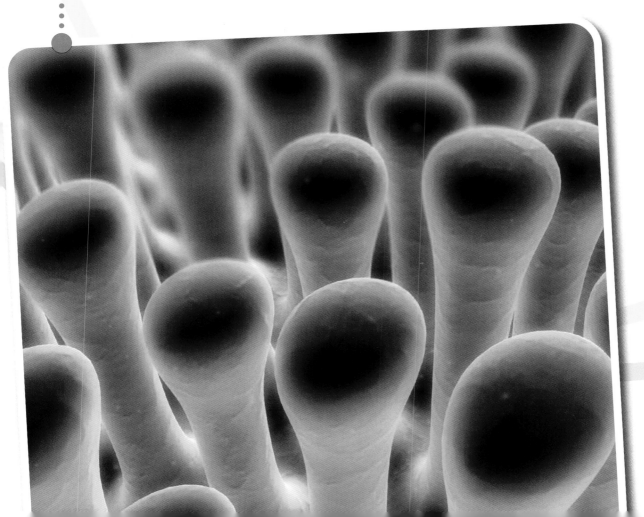

PROTEIN DE-LIVER-Y

Body Talk

Your body cannot store protein. This means that you have to eat protein every day to provide your body with the amino acids it needs.

Blood stocked with nutrients flows from the small intestine straight to the liver. Among other things, the liver controls the amounts of each amino acid and other nutrients that are taken in the blood to the rest of the body.

Blood reaches the liver from your heart as well as from the small intestine. This blood is already rich in oxygen. The liver then processes and adds all the nutrients the body needs.

Your kidneys continually produce urine, which is stored in the bladder.

Chemical factory

The liver is like a mini chemistry laboratory in your body. It can process nutrients into different chemicals and also acts as a store if it receives too many nutrients. The liver cannot store amino acids, so it may change one amino acid into another. It can also change amino acids into sugar to provide extra energy for the cells. The liver changes the rest of the excess protein into urea. This waste protein ends up in your urine.

Urea is carried in your blood to your kidneys. The kidneys filter the blood and separate out urea along with excess water and salts. These mix together to form urine, which trickles down to the bladder. When your bladder is full–that is a sign that you need to go to the toilet!

Did you know?

If part of the liver is removed for medical reasons, the rest of the liver carries on working and soon grows back to the size it was.

Blood flows through a lot of tiny tubes inside the liver.

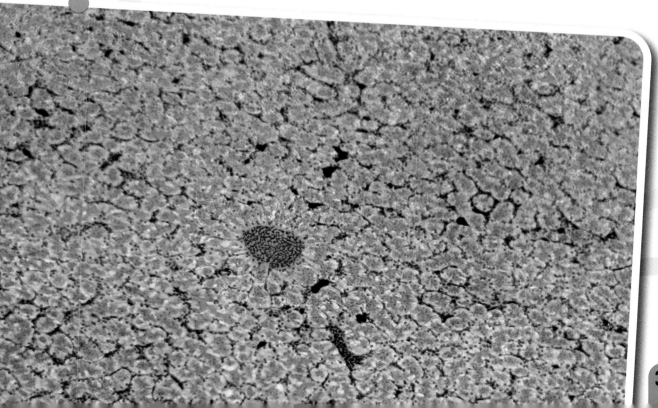

Body Talk

Hemophilia is a disease in which the blood does not make enough of the proteins that form **clots**. If a person with hemophilia is cut, it is hard to stop the bleeding. People with the disease will often have deep bruises on their bodies and painful, swollen joints that are caused by bleeding inside the body. Drugs can help make the blood produce more protein, but it is still important to be very careful not to get hurt.

Into the cells

Blood, packed with amino acids, flows from the liver back to the heart and then to every cell in the body. Each cell takes the amino acids it needs to build its own proteins.

Tsar Nicholas II of Russia suffered from hemophilia. Hemophilia is very rare and affects only males. It is, however, carried by females and can be passed on to their children.

Each cell is covered with a kind of skin called a **membrane**, which controls what passes into and out of the cell. The **nucleus** controls the whole cell. It contains genes (made of protein) that tell the cell exactly what to do. Ribosomes are the parts of the cell that assemble the amino acids to make proteins, which are then stored in the Golgi complex.

Proteins at work

The enzyme that digests protein is made in the pancreas. Other digestive enzymes are made in the liver and in the walls of the small intestine. The blood itself uses amino acids to build new proteins. One of these is fibrin, the protein that helps to make blood clot and stop wounds from bleeding.

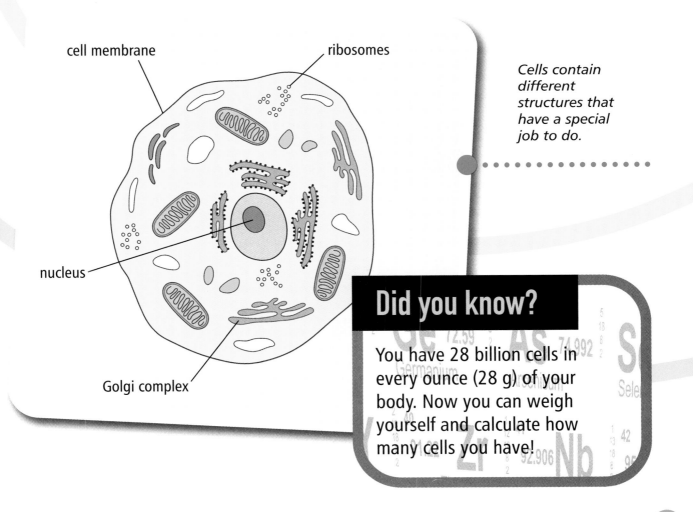

cell membrane

ribosomes

nucleus

Golgi complex

Cells contain different structures that have a special job to do.

Did you know?

You have 28 billion cells in every ounce (28 g) of your body. Now you can weigh yourself and calculate how many cells you have!

Waste proteins

As the cells carry out their work, they produce waste in the form of proteins. Dealing with waste proteins is another job for the liver. It changes them into urea, which leaves your body as a liquid called urine.

The kidneys

Urea is carried in your blood to your kidneys. You have two kidneys, one on each side of your body near your waist. Each kidney is about four inches (10 cm) long and two inches (5 cm) wide. The kidneys carry out several important jobs. They balance the amount of salt and water in the blood, and they clean the blood by getting rid of waste urea. The kidneys also soak up any useful nutrients back into the blood.

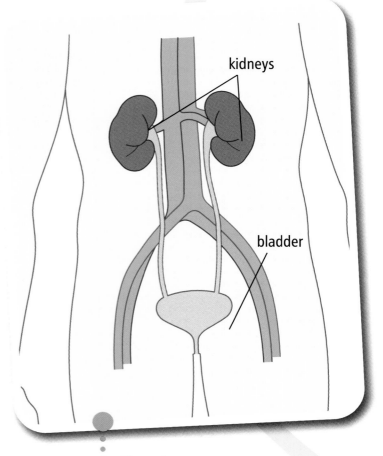

The urinary system consists of all the organs and tubes that work together to make and get rid of urine waste. The main parts of the urinary system are the kidneys, bladder, and the tubes that connect them.

Did you know?

You probably produce about three pints (1.4 l) of urine a day, depending on how much water you drink.

Making urine

The kidneys work by filtering the blood and separating out urea along with excess water and salts. These mix together to form urine, which trickles down to the bladder, where it is stored. When your bladder is full, you feel the need to pee, and the urine passes out of your body.

Body Talk

Kidneys that do not work properly do not filter out all the urea from the blood. It can leave a person feeling achy and very tired. In serious cases, a kidney transplant may be required. Surgery replaces the nonfunctioning kidney with a healthy one from another person. Waiting for a suitable kidney to become available can take a long time. In the meantime, the person waiting undergoes dialysis, which means being connected to a machine that cleans the blood.

Drinking water is very important. Water keeps our bodies hydrated and also helps to flush out waste proteins.

FOOD ALLERGIES AND SPECIAL DIETS

Many people decide not to eat certain foods. People who avoid meat, and sometimes fish, are called vegetarians. Vegans go one step further. They do not eat any foods that comes from animals, including milk and eggs. Other people avoid certain foods, such as shellfish and pork, for religious reasons. People with food allergies must avoid certain foods because their bodies react to chemicals in the food.

This salad contains no food that comes from animals.

Farmers raise livestock such as goats for meat and products such as milk to drink and make cheese. Vegans choose not to consume these products.

No meat!

Vegetarians can combine plant proteins with eggs, cheese, or other dairy foods to get all the nutrients they need. Vegans have to be more careful, however. Animal foods contain certain vitamins that are difficult to get from purely plant foods alone. Vegetarians and vegans also have to check ingredients carefully because many foods contain hidden animal products. People who go a long time without eating meat may find that they become unable to eat meat without feeling sick.

Allergies

For some people even a small amount of certain proteins is too much! These are people who suffer from food allergies, or are **intolerant** of certain foods. When they eat these foods, their bodies react as though the foods were harmful.

I am vegetarian and can eat anything I like, except meat and chicken. I eat fish sometimes.

I am a vegan, and I stay really healthy by eating a lot of beans, grains, and vegetables.

Allergic reactions

People can react in a variety of ways to food allergies. They may feel sick and vomit. They may get stomach cramps, diarrhea, an itchy skin rash, a runny nose, itchy eyes, or may find it difficult to breathe.

Body Talk

No bread, thanks! Some people are allergic to gluten. This is the protein in wheat and some other cereals. If they eat gluten, they get violent stomachaches, swollen bellies, and diarrhea.

Shellfish, such as lobsters, may look delicious, but they can be fatal if eaten by someone who is allergic to them.

Try this...

Plan a day's food for someone who is allergic to gluten and dairy foods. What foods can they eat? Try to create three meals without gluten or dairy.

Most food allergies are caused by the proteins in certain foods. Nuts, eggs, shellfish, and wheat are some of the most common food allergies. People who are allergic have to avoid eating even a tiny amount of the problem food or foods. This means that they have to check the ingredients on food labels before they eat them.

Few people are allergic to dairy foods, but for many people, eating dairy foods makes them feel sick. This is often called being lactose intolerant.

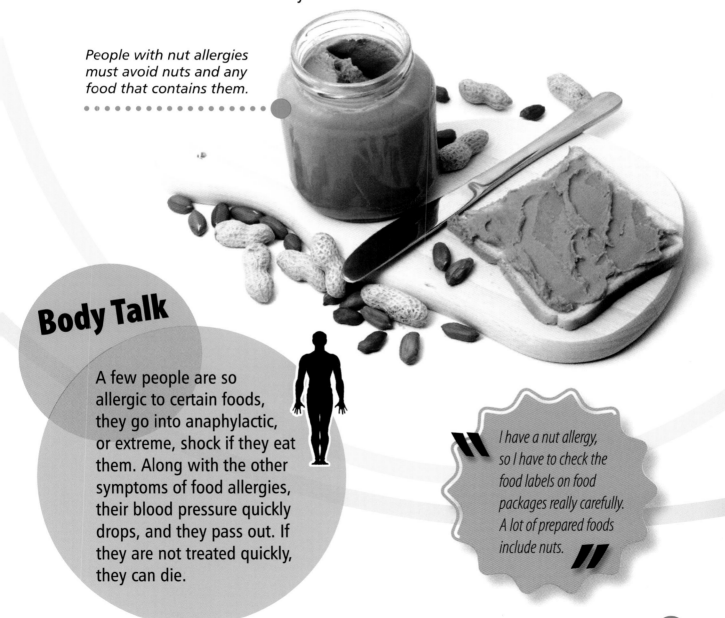

People with nut allergies must avoid nuts and any food that contains them.

Body Talk

A few people are so allergic to certain foods, they go into anaphylactic, or extreme, shock if they eat them. Along with the other symptoms of food allergies, their blood pressure quickly drops, and they pass out. If they are not treated quickly, they can die.

I have a nut allergy, so I have to check the food labels on food packages really carefully. A lot of prepared foods include nuts.

FOOD FACTS AND STATS

The amount of protein in food is measured in two ways. It is either measured directly or it is measured as the amount of food needed to give an equivalent amount of protein. Since all food contains a lot of water, the equivalent amounts are higher than the actual protein amounts.

Recommended daily amounts of equivalent protein amounts

	Age in years	Weight
Young children	2–3	2 oz (55 g)
	4–8	4 oz (85 g)
Girls	9–18	5 oz (140 g)
Boys	9–13	5 oz (140 g)
	14–18	6 oz (170 g)
Women	19–30	5.5 oz (155 g)
	Over 31	5 oz (140 g)
Men	19–30	6.5 oz (184 g)
	31–50	6 oz (170 g)
	Over 50	5.5 oz (155 g)

Recommended amounts of actual protein
Men	2 oz (55 g)
Women	1.5 oz (45 g)
Children aged 9–13	1.5 oz (45 g)

Amount of equivalent protein in different foods
1 oz (28 g) of lean meat, poultry, or fish gives 1 oz (28 g) of equivalent protein

1 cup (240 ml) of cooked dry pulses (beans, chickpeas, lentils) gives 2 oz (55 g) of equivalent protein

1 egg gives 1 oz (28 g) of equivalent protein

1 oz (28 g) of nuts or seeds gives 2 oz (55 g) of equivalent protein

Recommended daily amounts of different kinds of food for children aged 9 to 13
Grains	5 oz (140 g) (girls) 6 oz (170 g) (boys)
Vegetables	2 cups (475 ml) (girls) 2.5 cups (600 ml) (boys)
Fruit	1.5 cups (350 ml)
Milk	3 cups (700 ml)
Meat and beans	5 oz (140 g)
Oils	5 teaspoons (25 ml)

Comparing calories
Energy in food is measured in calories. This is what 1 oz (28 g) gives:
Carbohydrate	105 calories
Protein	112 calories
Fat	252 calories

Examples of amount of actual protein in certain foods
4 oz (113 g) of chicken contains about 1.25 oz (35.6 g) of protein

7 oz (200 g) of tuna steak contains 2 oz (55 g) of protein

2 oz (55 g) of cheese contains nearly 0.5 oz (13 g) of protein

1 glass of milk contains about 0.2 oz (6 g) of protein

1 egg contains about 0.2 oz (6 g) of protein

GLOSSARY

albumen White of an egg

amino acid Natural compound that is part of protein

antibodies Proteins in the blood that destroy harmful germs in the body

carbohydrate Sugar or starch that is the main source of energy

cartilage Tough, flexible material

chemical reaction Change that happens when chemicals react with each other

chyme Digestive juice

clot The thickening and sticking together of a liquid to make a lump

collagen Fiber-rich protein

digestive system Body part that turns food into elements your body needs

enzyme Protein that helps to break down food in your system

equivalent Equal to

esophagus Muscular tube that brings food from your throat to your stomach

famine Extreme lack of food in an area

germ Small group of cells; center part of a plant, often containing nutrients

hemoglobin Blood cell containing iron; the iron gives the blood its red color

hormone Chemical released by cells or glands that controls processes in other parts of the body

intestine Long tube in the body through which food passes after leaving the stomach

intolerant Unable to eat certain foods because the body reacts badly to them

keratin Very tough protein that makes up your hair, nails, and skin

legume Pod, such as a pea or bean

membrane Thin layer of tissue that covers a surface

molecule Smallest part of a substance

nucleus Center part

nutrient Healthy source of nourishment

pancreas Gland behind the stomach

puberty Phase of life when children's bodies change to become adults

saliva Watery mixture in the mouth

trans fat An unhealthy fat made by heating vegetable oil in hydrogen gas

FURTHER READING

Further Reading

Sayer, Dr. Melissa, *Too Fat? Too thin? The Healthy Eating Guidebook*. Crabtree Publishing, 2009.

Doeden, Matt, *Eat Right*, Lerner, 2009.

Gardner, Robert, *Health Science Projects about Nutrition*. Enslow Publishers, 2002.

Royston, Angela. *Proteins for a Healthy Body*. Heinemann-Raintree, 2009.

Internet

Your Digestive System
http://kidshealth.org/kid/htbw/digestive_system.html

Learning about Proteins
http://kidshealth.org/kid/stay_healthy/
  body/protein.html

Your Gross and Cool Body
http://yucky.discovery.com/flash/body/
  pg000126.html

Try this...

Consider keeping a food journal. Write down everything you eat for an entire week. How much protein did you eat? Was it more or less than you needed?

INDEX